THE BEATLES

FOR SOLO MANDOLIN

20 CLASSICS ARRANGED FOR CHORD - MELODY MANDOLIN

T0039930

Cover photo by David Redfern / Getty Images
Arranged by Bill LaFleur

ISBN 978-1-4803-9306-6

7777 W. BLUEMOUND RD. P.O. BOX 13819 MILWAUKEE, WI 53213

Visit Hal Leonard Online at
www.halleonard.com

All You Need Is Love

Words and Music by John Lennon and Paul McCartney

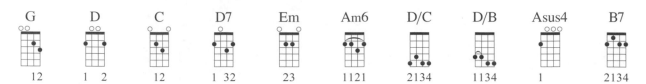

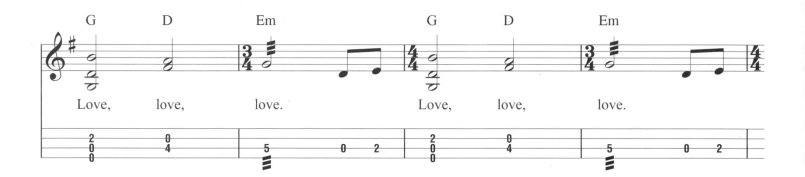

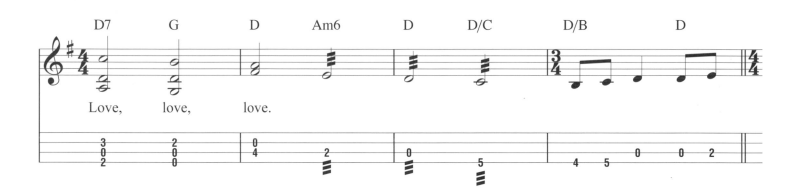

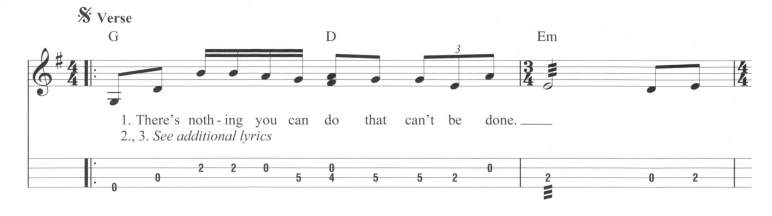

1. There's noth-ing you can do that can't be done. _____
2., 3. *See additional lyrics*

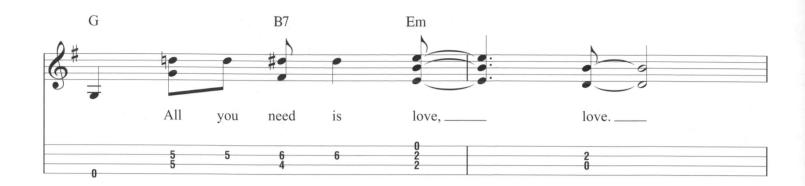

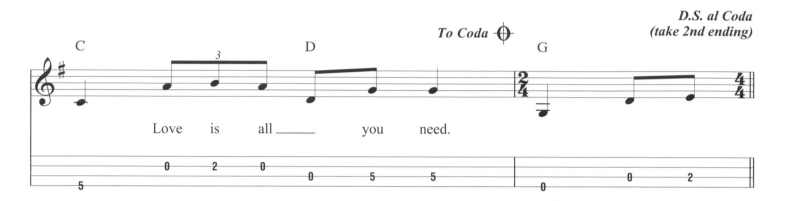

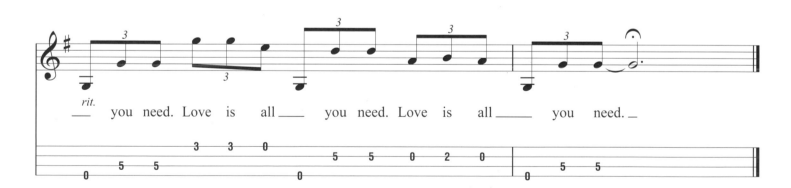

Additional Lyrics

2. Nothing you can make that can't be made.
   No one you can save that can't be saved.
   Nothing you can do, but you can learn how to be you in time.
   It's easy.

3. There's nothing you can know that isn't known.
   Nothing you can see that isn't shown.
   There's nowhere you can be that isn't where you're meant to be.
   It's easy.

Blackbird

Words and Music by John Lennon and Paul McCartney

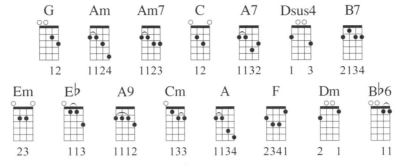

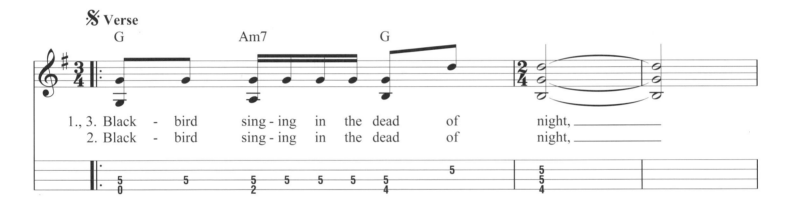

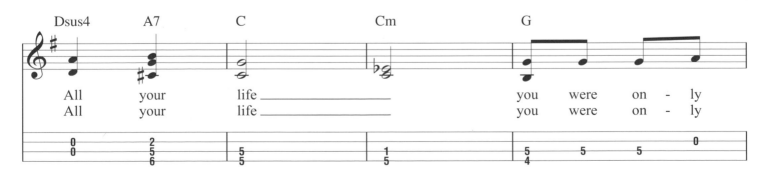

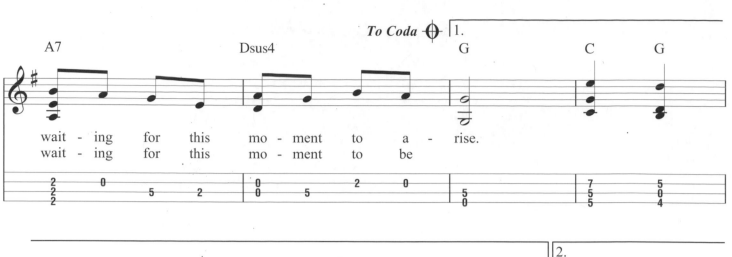

waiting for this moment to a - rise.
wait - ing for this mo - ment to be

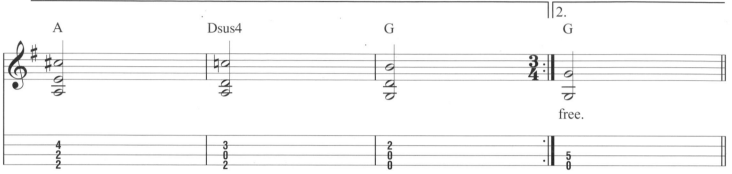

free.

Bridge

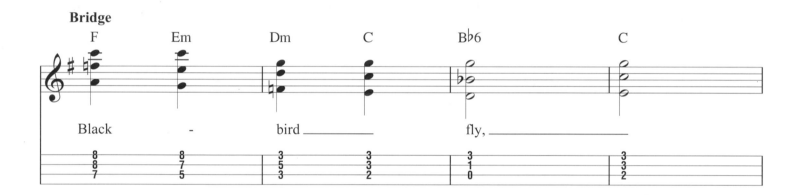

Black - bird _____ fly, _____

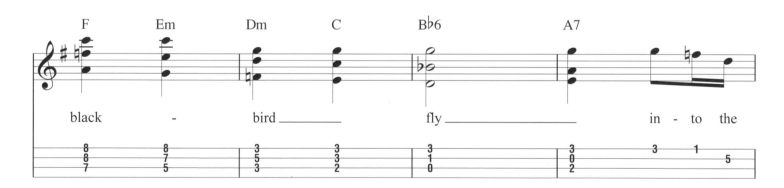

black - bird _____ fly _____ in - to the

Interlude

light of a dark, black night. ____

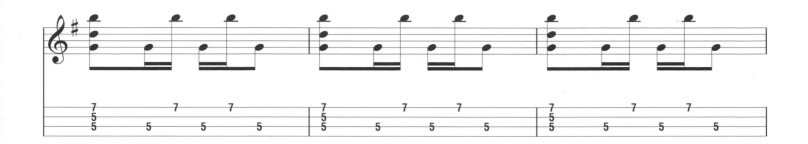

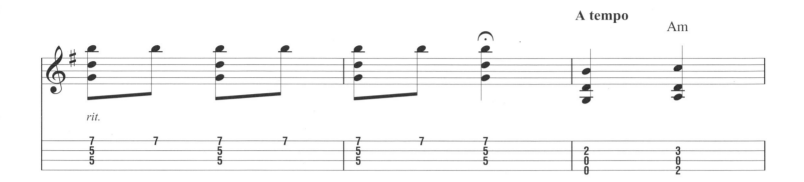

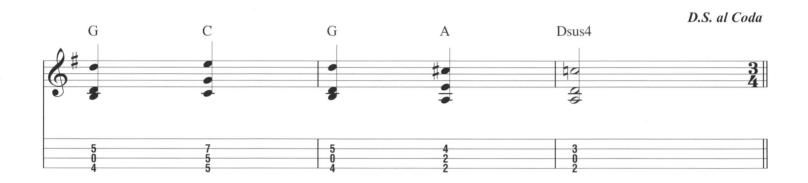

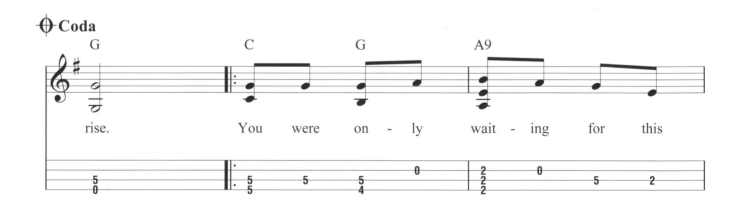

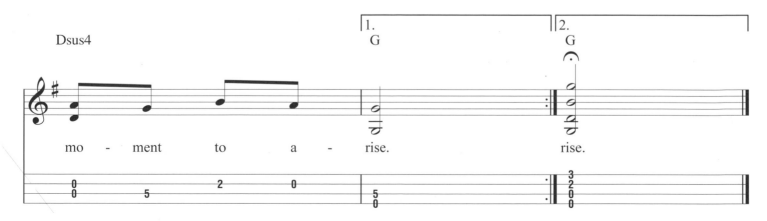

Can't Buy Me Love

Words and Music by John Lennon and Paul McCartney

Additional Lyrics

2. I'll give you all I've got to give if you say you love me too.
   I may not have a lot to give, but what I got I'll give to you.
   'Cause I don't care too much for money, 'cause money can't buy me love.

3., 4. Say you don't need no diamond rings and I'll be satisfied.
   Tell me that you want the kind of things that money just can't buy.
   I don't care too much for money, money can't buy me love.

Get Back

Words and Music by John Lennon and Paul McCartney

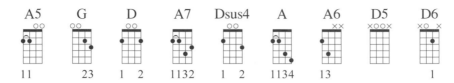

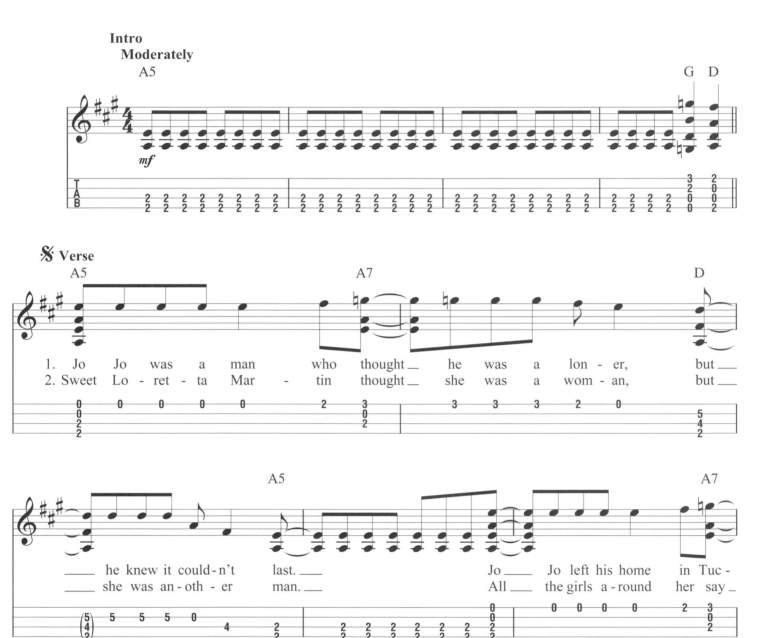

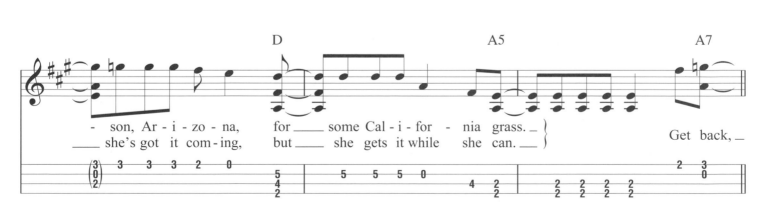

Chorus

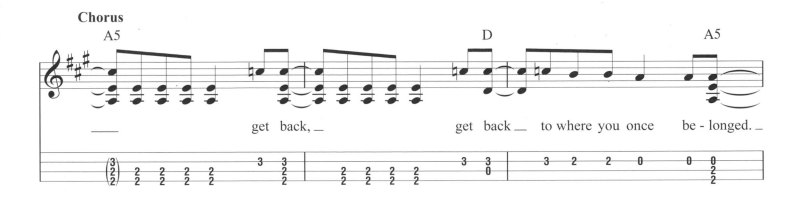

get back, __ get back __ to where you once be - longed. __

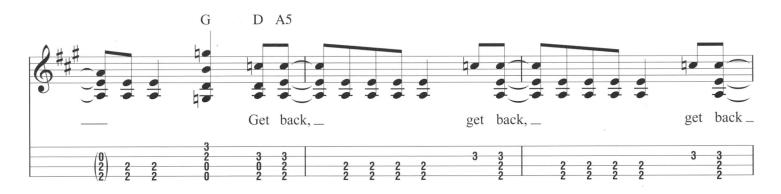

Get back, __ get back, __ get back __

D.S. al Coda

__ to where you once be - longed. __

Coda

Outro

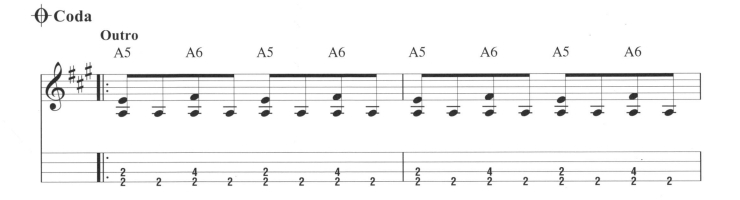

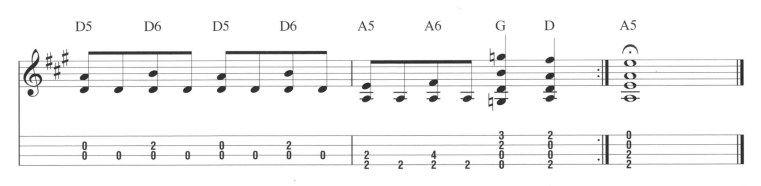

Eight Days a Week

Words and Music by John Lennon and Paul McCartney

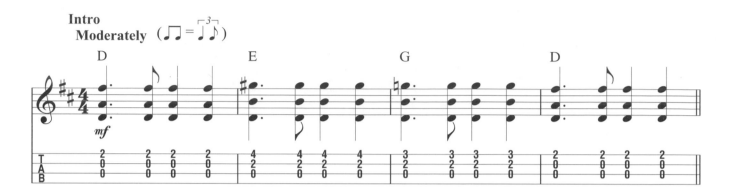

ain't got noth-in but   love, babe, ___   eight days a week. _____

Bridge

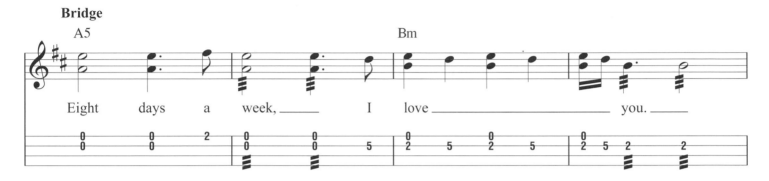

Eight   days   a   week, ___   I   love _____ you. ___

1st time, D.S.
(no repeat)
2nd time, D.S. al Coda
(no repeat)

Eight   days   a   week   is   not e - nough to   show I   care. __

⊕ **Coda**   **Outro**

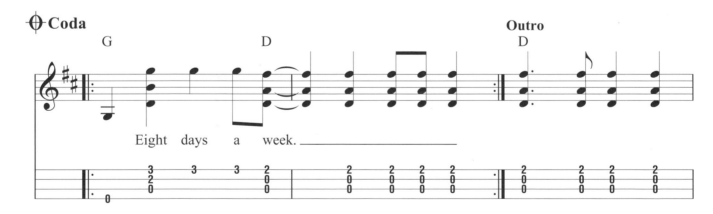

Eight days a week. _____

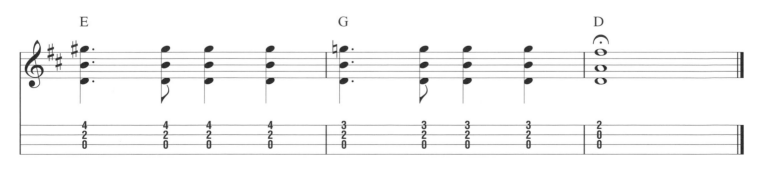

Here Comes the Sun

Words and Music by George Harrison

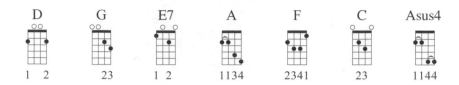

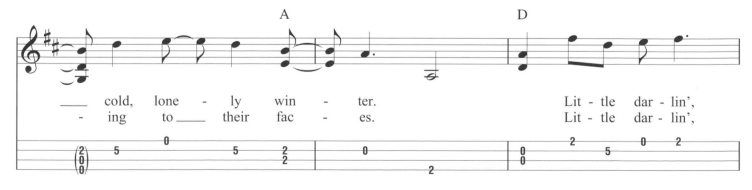

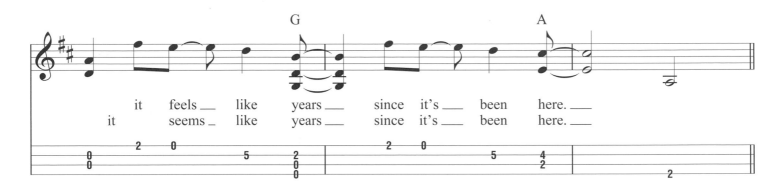

it feels ___ like years ___ since it's ___ been here. ___
it seems ___ like years ___ since it's ___ been here. ___

Chorus

Here comes ___ the sun, ___ doo, 'n' doo, doo. Here comes ___ the sun ___

___ 'n' I ___ say, it's al - right.

To Coda ⊕

1.

2.

Bridge

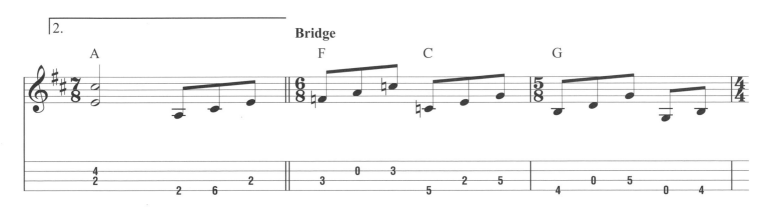

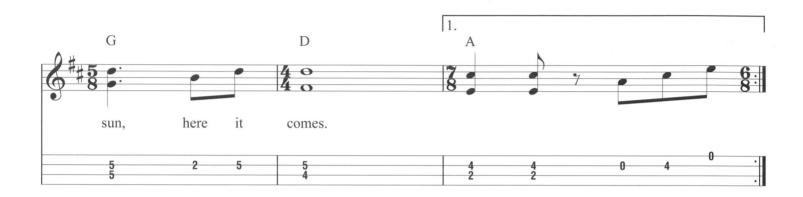

Sun,   sun,

sun,   here   it   comes.

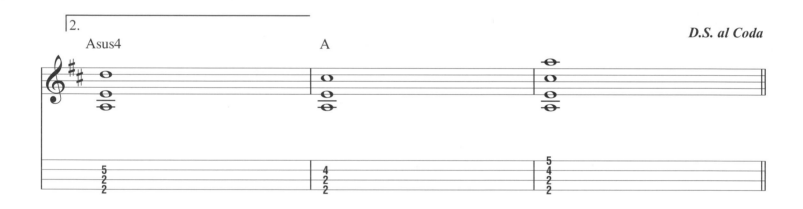

D.S. al Coda

rit.

Additional Lyrics

3. Little darlin', I feel that ice is slowly melting.
Little darlin', it seems like years since it's been clear.

Hey Jude

Words and Music by John Lennon and Paul McCartney

*Tremolo top note only, throughout.

D.S. al Coda
(take 2nd ending)

$\oplus$ **Coda 1**

D.S. al Coda 2

Additional Lyrics

2. Hey, Jude, don't be afraid. You were made to go out and get her.
   The minute you let her under your skin, then you begin to make it better.

3. Hey, Jude don't let me down. You have found her now go and get her.
   Remember to let her into your heart, then you can start to make it better.

4. Hey, Jude, don't make it bad, take a sad song and make it better.
   Remember to let her under your skin, then you begin to make it better.

I Feel Fine

Words and Music by John Lennon and Paul McCartney

Intro
Moderately

Verse

1. Ba - by's good to me, ___ you know, _ she's hap - py as can be, ___ you know, _ she
2.-5. *See additional lyrics*

said so.   I'm in love with her ___ and I ___ feel _

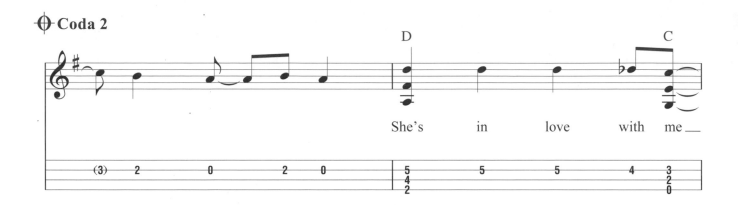

Additional lyrics

2., 4. Baby says she's mine, you know, she tells me all the time, you know, she said so.
I'm in love with her and I feel fine.

3., 5. That her baby buys her things, you know, he buys her diamond rings, you know, she said so.
She's in love with me and I feel fine.

I Saw Her Standing There

Words and Music by John Lennon and Paul McCartney

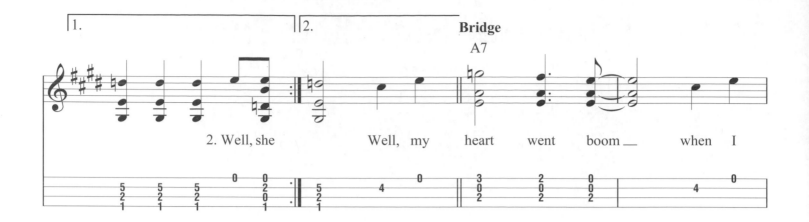

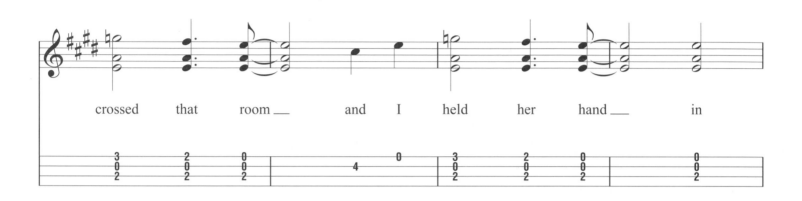

Coda

Additional Lyrics

2. Well, she looked at me and I, I could see
   That before too long I'd fall in love with her.
   She wouldn't dance with another, oo,
   When I saw her standing there.

3., 4. Oh, we danced through the night and we held each other tight,
   And before too long I fell in love with her.
   Now, I'll never dance with another, oo,
   When I saw her standing there.

I Will

Words and Music by John Lennon and Paul McCartney

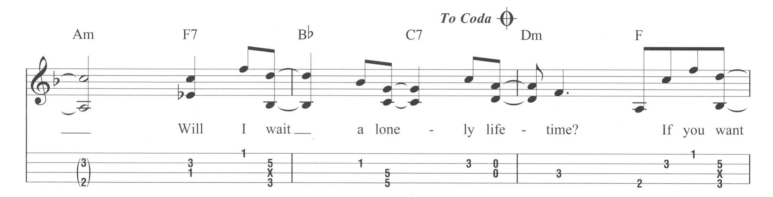

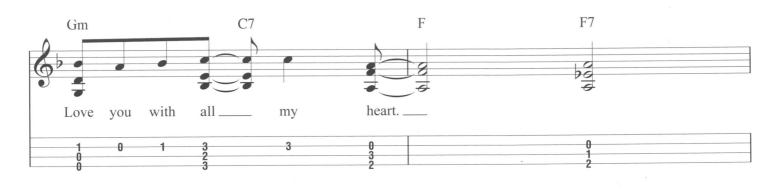

Love you with all — my heart. —

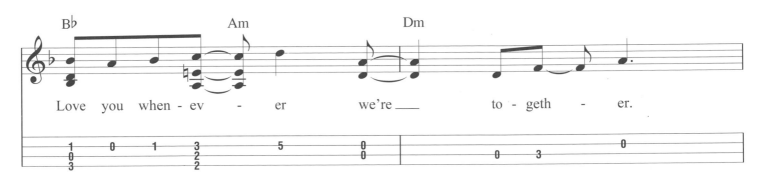

Love you when - ev - er we're — to - geth - er.

D.S. al Coda

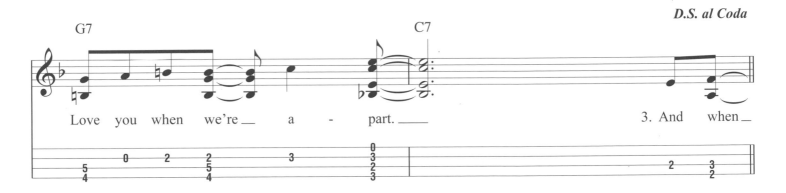

Love you when we're — a - part. — 3. And when —

⊕ **Coda**

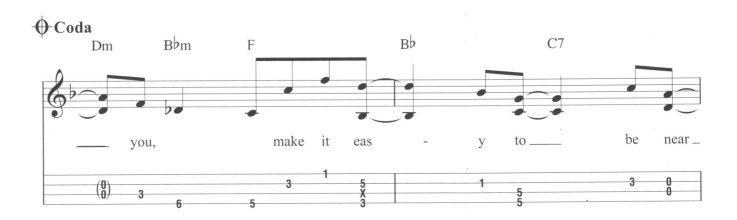

— you, make it eas - y to — be near —

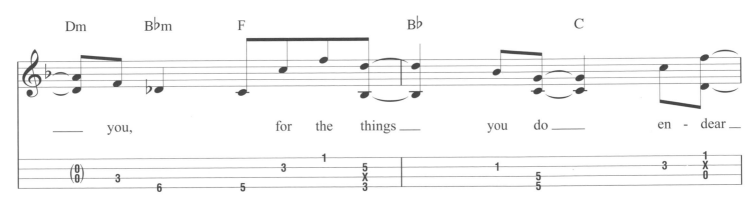

— you, for the things — you do — en - dear —

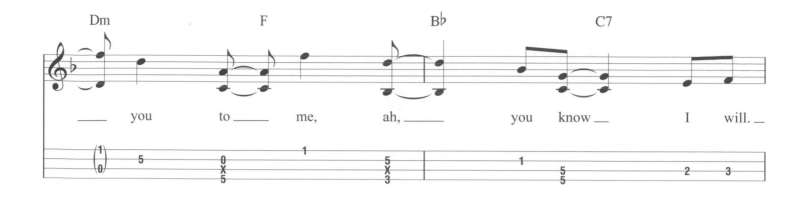

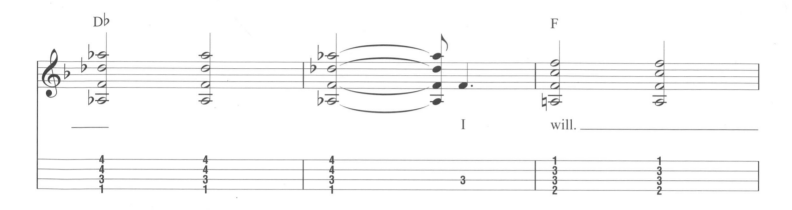

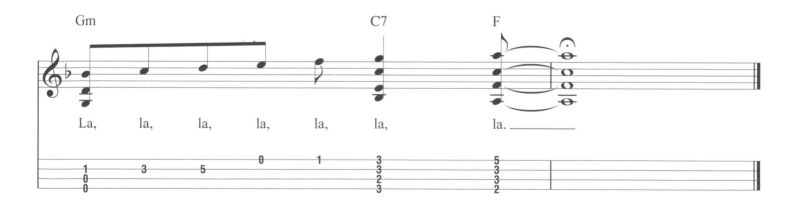

Additional Lyrics

2. For if I ever saw you, I didn't catch your name.
   But it never really mattered, I will always feel the same.

3. And when at last I find you, your song will fill the air.
   Sing it loud so I can hear you...

In My Life

Words and Music by John Lennon and Paul McCartney

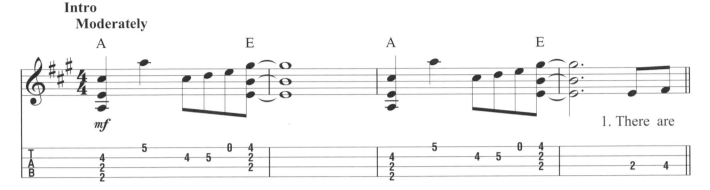

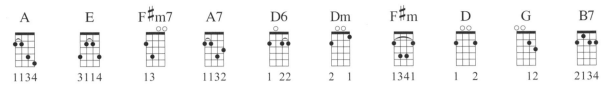

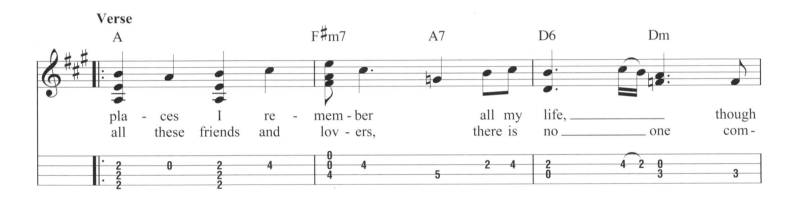

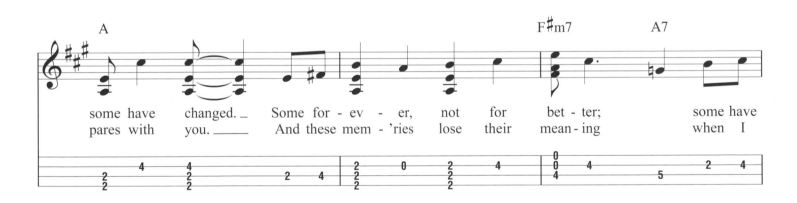

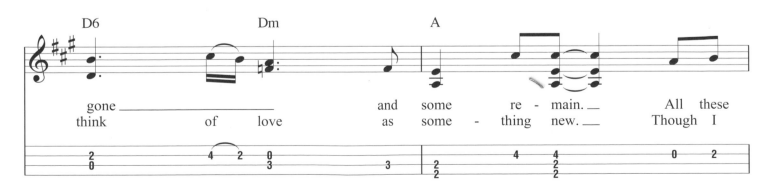

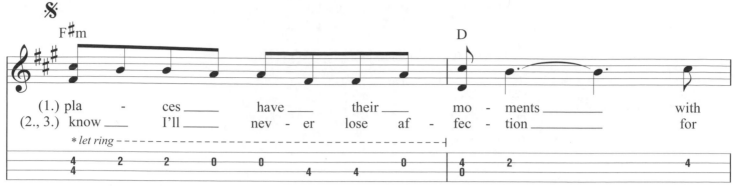

%

F#m   **D**

(1.) pla - ces ____ have ____ their ____ mo - ments _____ with
(2., 3.) know ____ I'll _____ nev - er lose af - fec - tion _____ for

let ring -

*Hold bottom note.

G   **A**

lov - ers and friends ____ I still can re - call. ____ Some are
peo - ple and things ____ that went ____ be - fore, ____ I

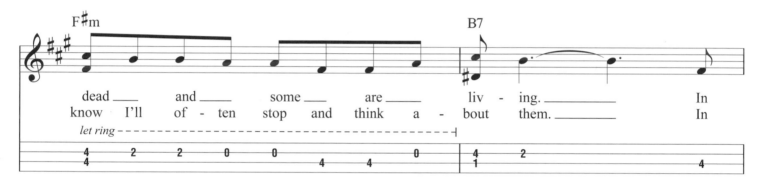

F#m   **B7**

dead ____ and ____ some ____ are ____ liv - ing. _____ In
know I'll of - ten stop and think a - bout them. _____ In

let ring -

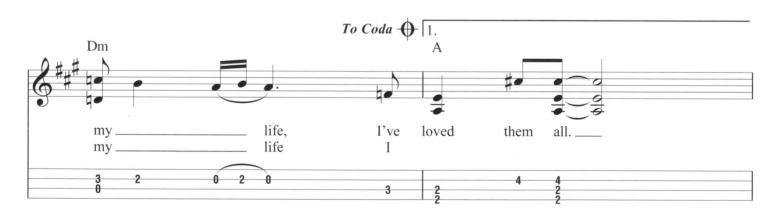

To Coda ⊕ |1.

Dm   **A**

my _____ life, I've loved them all. ____
my _____ life I

|2.

E   **A**

2. But of love you more.

Let It Be

Words and Music by John Lennon and Paul McCartney

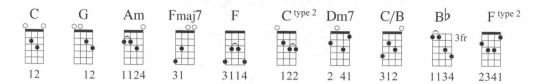

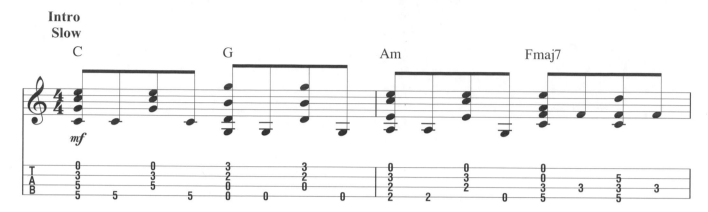

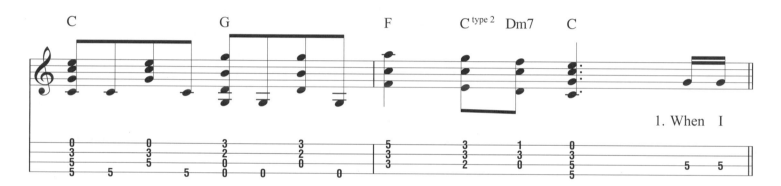

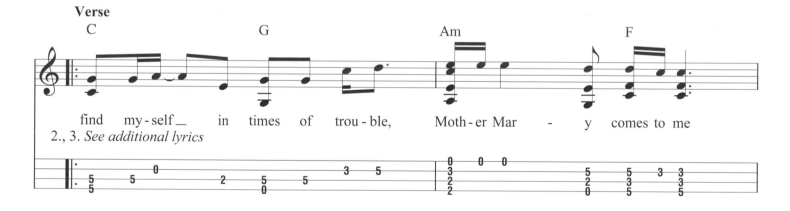

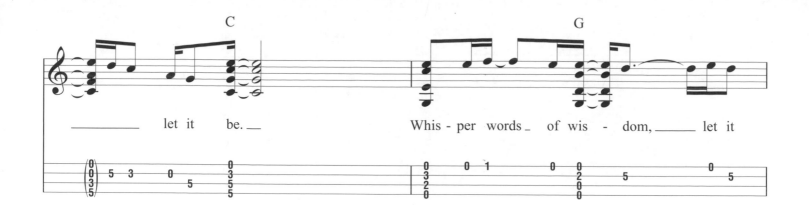

let it be. ___ Whis-per words ___ of wis - dom, ___ let it

To Coda ⊕

Interlude

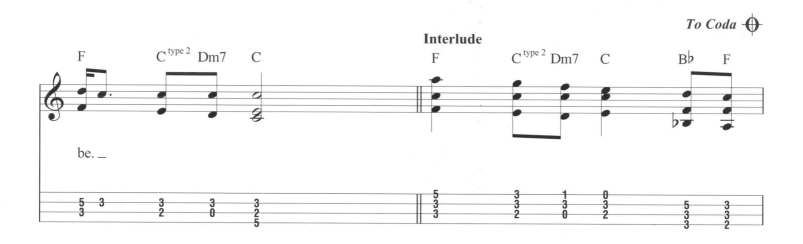

be. ___

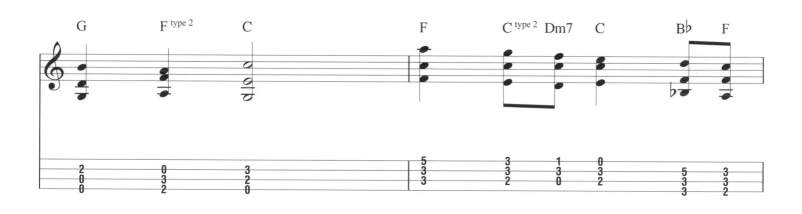

Mandolin Solo

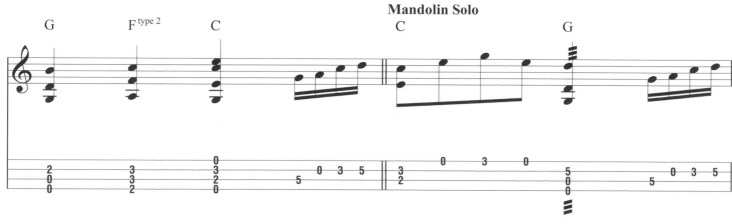

Additional Lyrics

2. And when the broken hearted people living in the world agree,
   There will be an answer, let it be.
   For though they may be parted, there is still a chance that they will see,
   There will be an answer, let it be.

4. And when the night is cloudy, there is still a light that shines on me,
   Shine until tomorrow, let it be.
   I wake up to the sound of music, Mother Mary comes to me
   Speaking words of wisdom, let it be.

Michelle

Words and Music by John Lennon and Paul McCartney

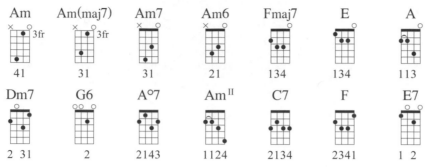

Intro
Moderately

1. Mi - chelle, ma belle, these are words that go to - geth - er

well, my Mi - chelle. 2., 3. Mi - chelle, ma belle,

*Tremolo top note only, throughout.

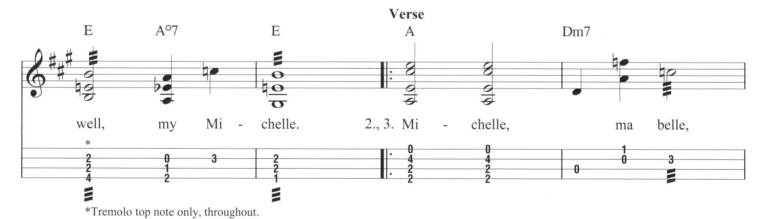

sont des mots qui vont tres bien en - semble, tres bien en - semble. ___ I

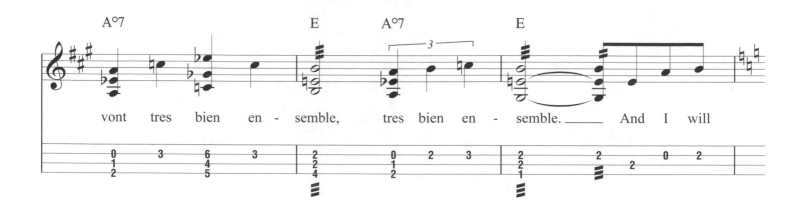

vont tres bien en - semble, tres bien en - semble. _____ And I will

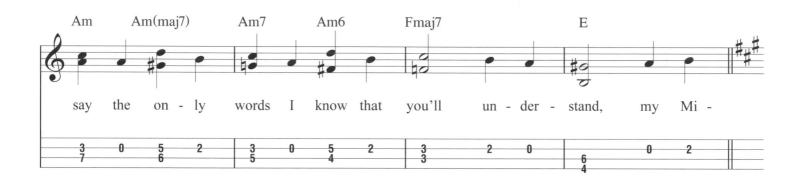

say the on - ly words I know that you'll un - der - stand, my Mi -

Outro

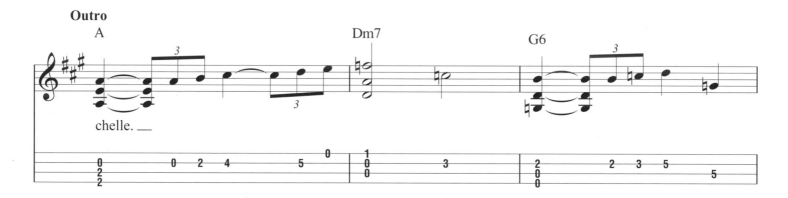

chelle. __

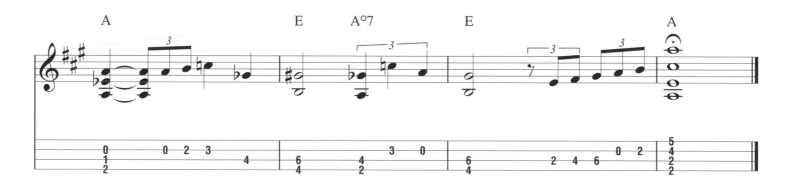

Additional Lyrics

2. I need to, I need to, I need to,
   I need to make you see,
   Oh, what you mean to me.
   Until I do, I'm hoping you will know what I mean.

3. I want you, I want you, I want you,
   I think you know by now.
   I'll get to you somehow.
   Until I do, I'm telling you so you'll understand.

Mother Nature's Son

Words and Music by John Lennon and Paul McCartney

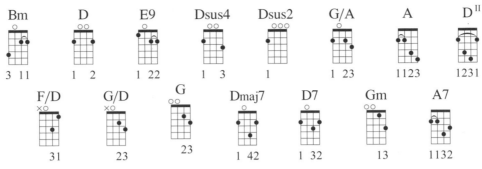

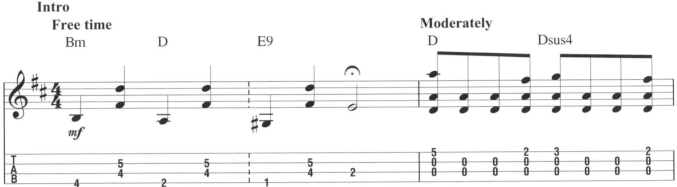

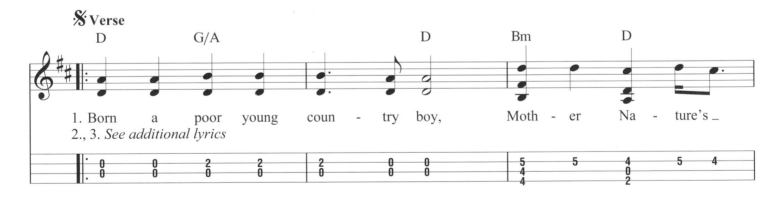

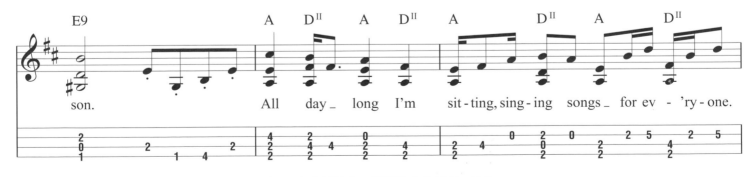

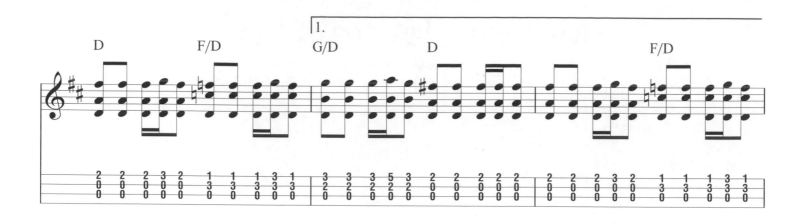

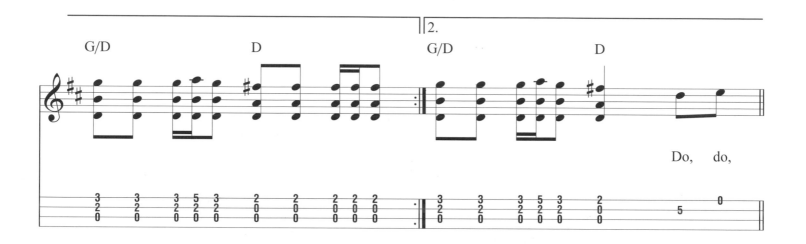

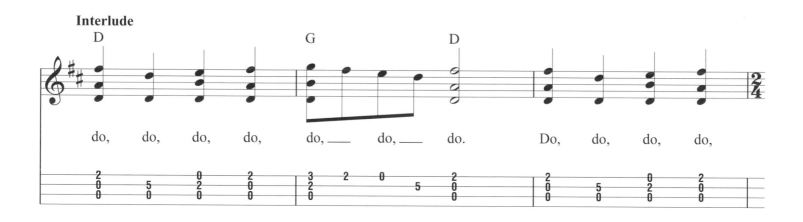

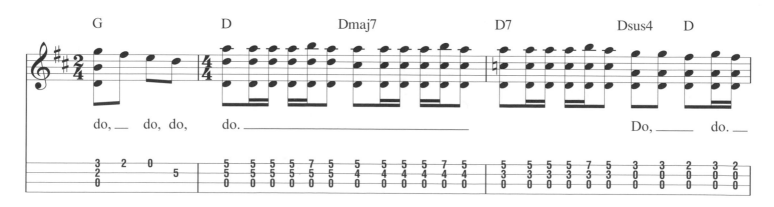

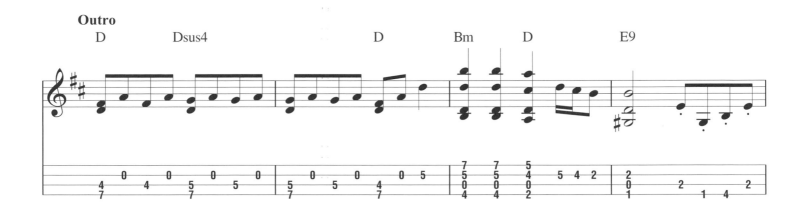

Outro

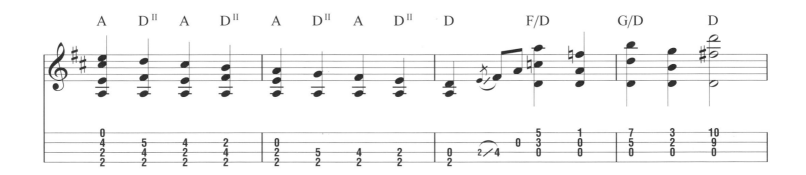

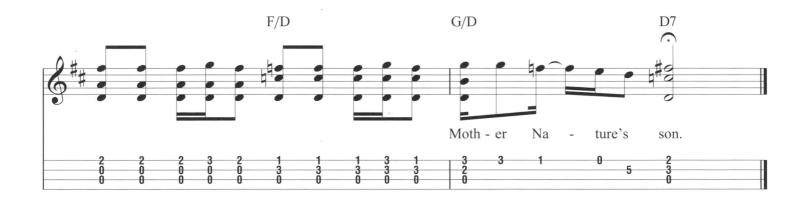

Moth - er   Na - ture's   son.

Additional Lyrics

2. Sit beside a mountain stream, see her waters rise.
   Listen to the pretty sound of music as she flies.

3. Find me in a field of grass, Mother Nature's son.
   Swaying daisies sing a lazy song beneath the sun.

Nowhere Man

Words and Music by John Lennon and Paul McCartney

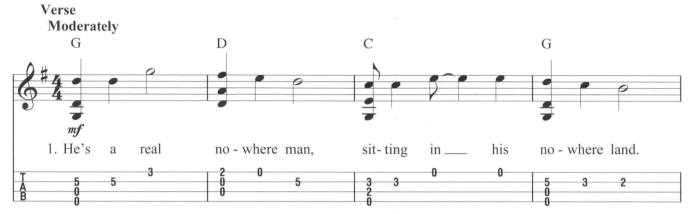

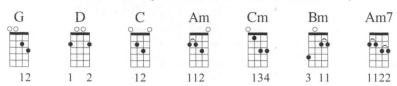

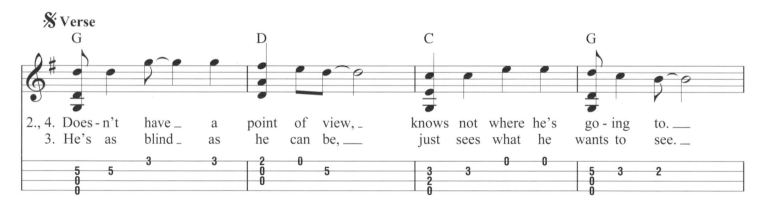

*Tremolo top note only, throughout

Bridge

_____ please lis - ten: you don't know ___ what _ you're miss - ing. ___ No - where _
_____ don't wor - ry, take your time, ___ don't hur - ry. ___ Leave it _____

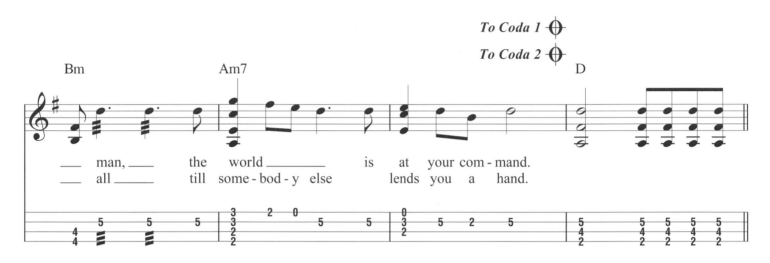

To Coda 1

To Coda 2

___ man, ___ the world _____ is at your com - mand.
___ all _____ till some - bod - y else lends you a hand.

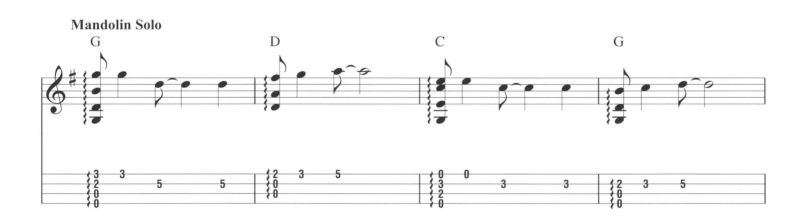

Mandolin Solo

D.S. al Coda 1

Harm.

Pitch: G

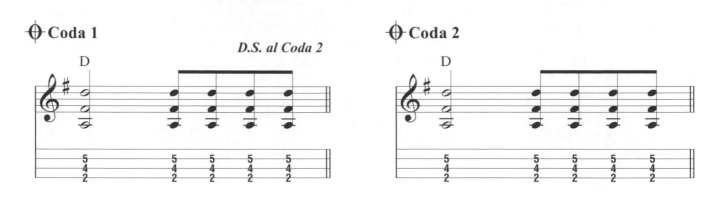

Verse

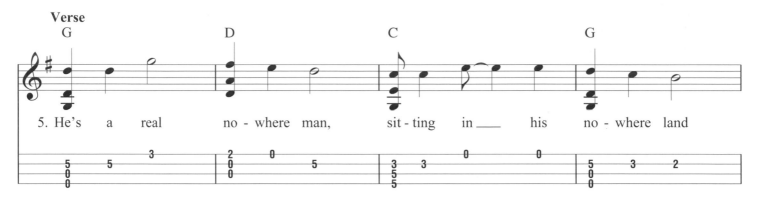

5. He's a real no - where man, sit - ting in ___ his no - where land

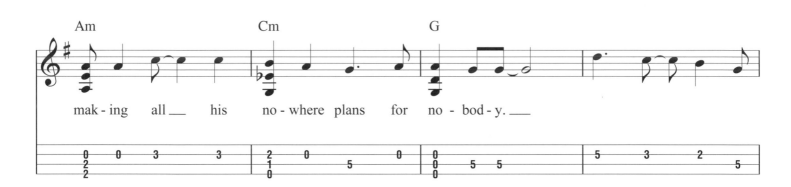

mak - ing all ___ his no - where plans for no - bod - y. ___

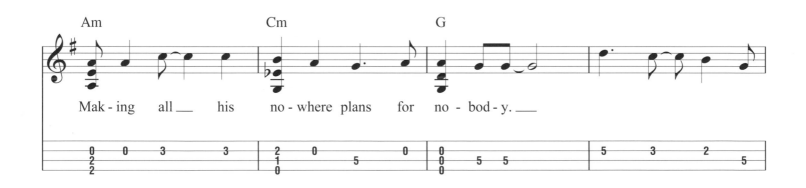

Mak - ing all ___ his no - where plans for no - bod - y. ___

Mak - ing all ___ his no - where plans for no - bod - y.

Strawberry Fields Forever

Words and Music by John Lennon and Paul McCartney

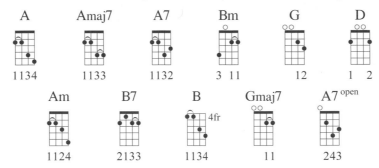

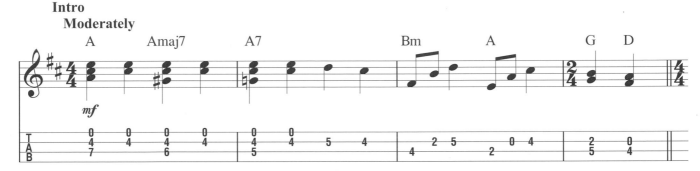

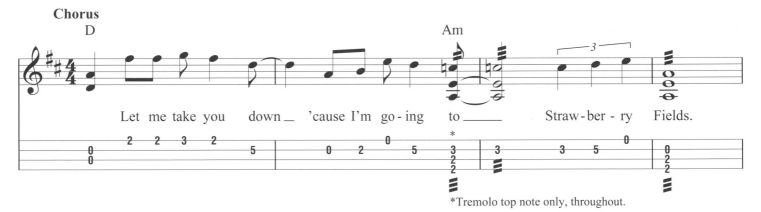

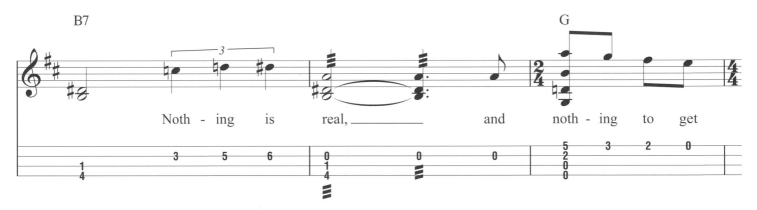

*Tremolo top note only, throughout.

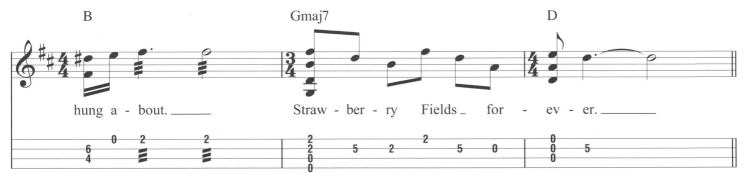

Verse

1. Liv - ing is eas - y with eyes closed,
2., 3. *See additional lyrics*

mis - un - der - stand - ing all you see._____ It's get - ting hard to be some-

one, but it all works out. It does - n't mat - ter much to me._____

Chorus

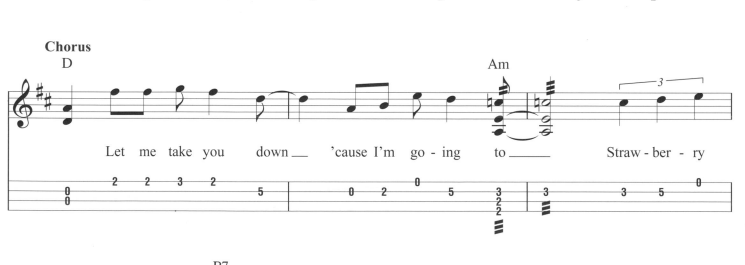

Let me take you down ____ 'cause I'm go - ing to _____ Straw - ber - ry

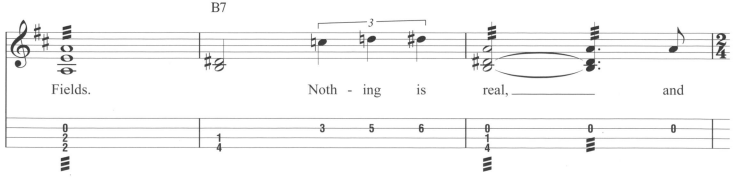

Fields. Noth - ing is real, _____ and

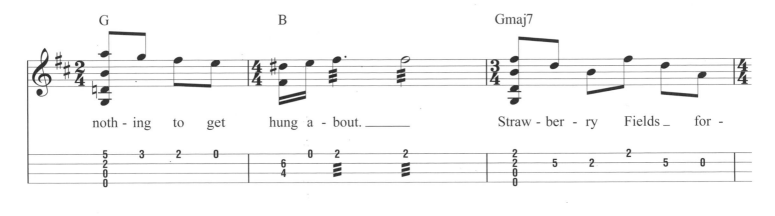

noth - ing to get hung a - bout. _____ Straw - ber - ry Fields _ for -

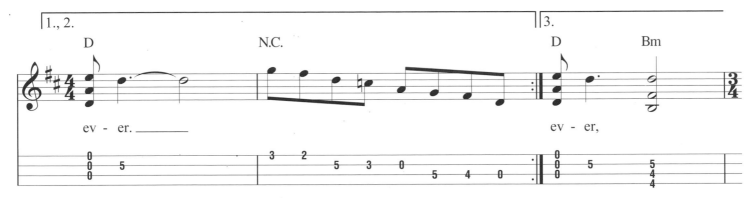

ev - er. _____ ev - er,

Straw - ber - ry Fields _ for - ev - er, _____ Straw - ber - ry Fields _ for -

ev - er. _____

Additional Lyrics

2. No one I think is in my tree,
   I mean it must be high or low.
   That is, you know, you can't tune in but it's all right,
   That is I think it's not too bad.

3. Always know, sometimes think it's me,
   But you know I know when it's a dream.
   I think a "No", will be a "Yes," but it's all wrong,
   That is, I think I disagree.

Twist and Shout

Words and Music by Bert Russell and Phil Medley

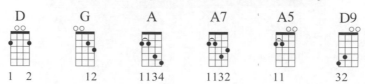

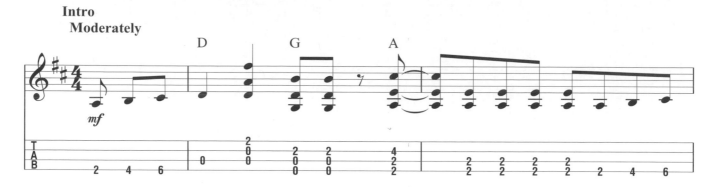

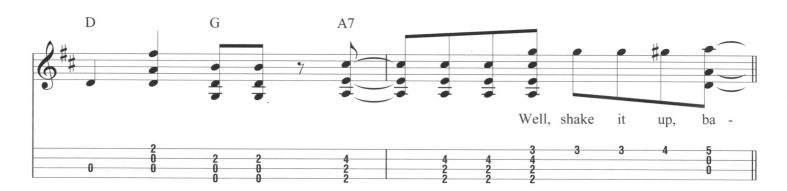

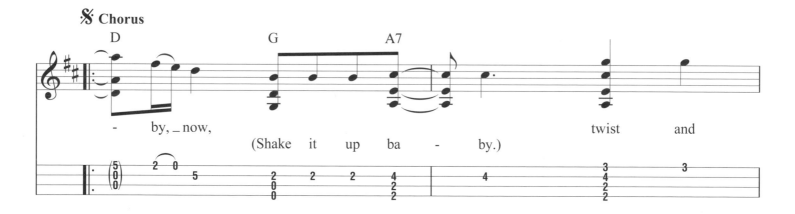

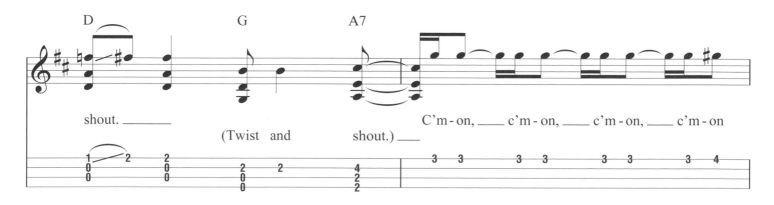

Additional Lyrics

2., 3.   You know you're a twisty little girl.
         (Twist little girl.)
         You know you twist so fine.
         (Twist so fine.)
         Come on and twist a little closer, now.
         (Twist a little closer.)
         And let me know that you're mine.
         (Let me know you're mine.)

We Can Work It Out

Words and Music by John Lennon and Paul McCartney

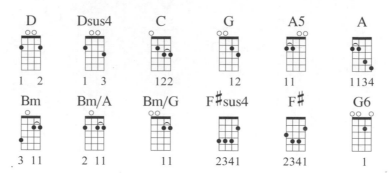

Verse
Moderately

1. Try to see it my way, do I have to keep on talk-ing

2., 3., 4. *See additional lyrics*

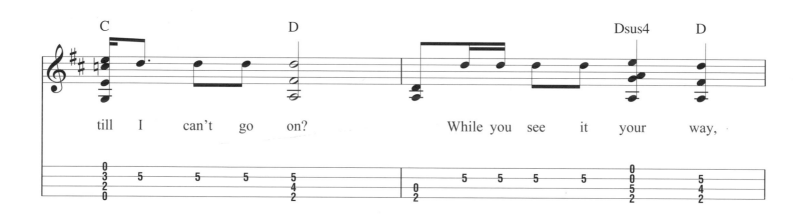

till I can't go on? While you see it your way,

run a risk of know-ing that our love may soon be gone. _____

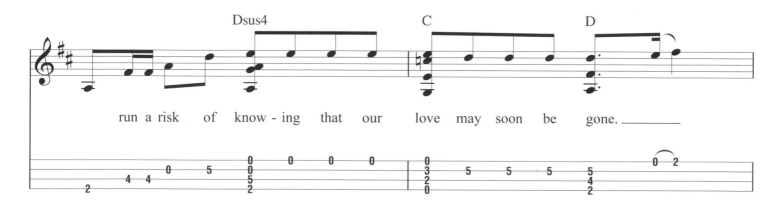

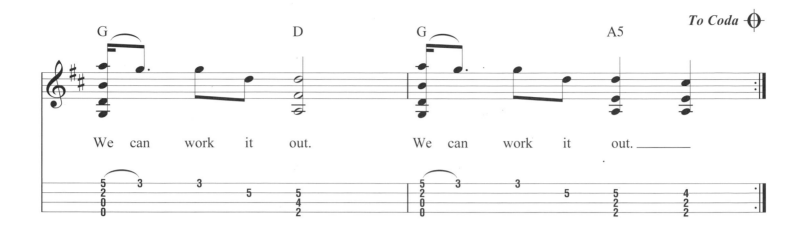

We can work it out. We can work it out. _____

Bridge

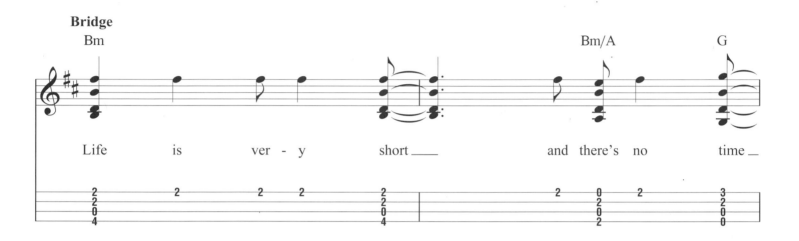

Life is ver - y short _____ and there's no time _

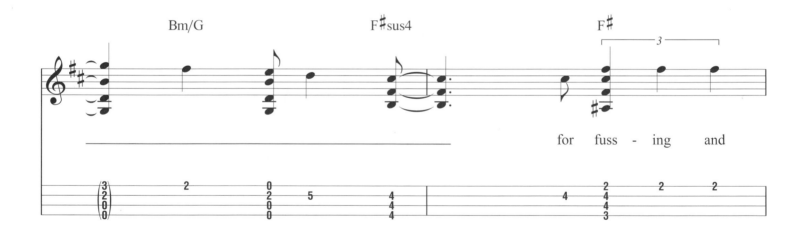

for fuss - ing and

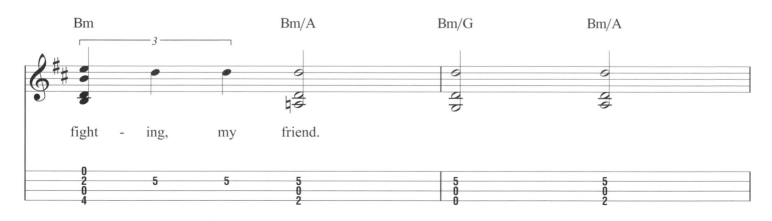

fight - ing, my friend.

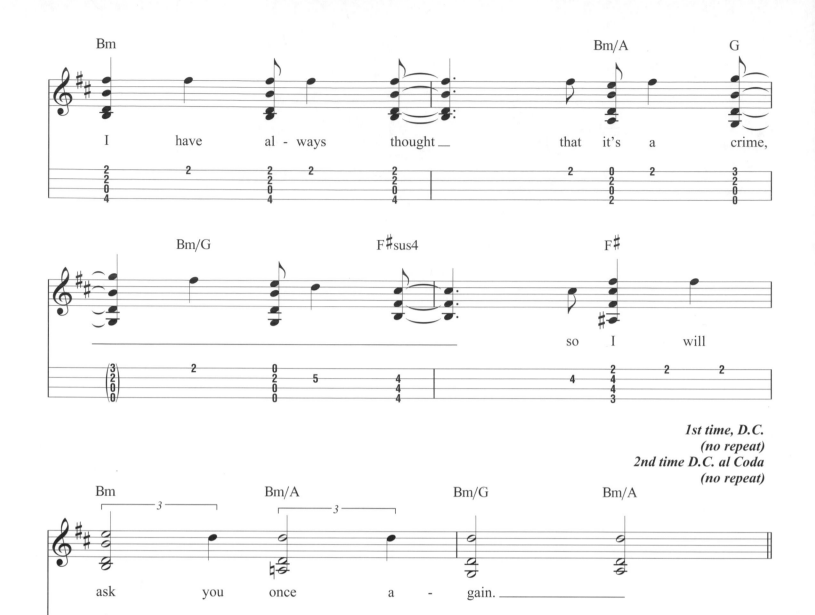

1st time, D.C.
(no repeat)
2nd time D.C. al Coda
(no repeat)

Additional Lyrics

2. Think of what you're saying,
   You can get it wrong and still you think that it's alright.
   Think of what I'm saying,
   We can work it out and get it straight, or say goodnight.

3., 4. Try to see it my way,
   Only time will tell if I am right or I am wrong.
   While you see it your way,
   There's a chance that we might fall apart before too long.

With a Little Help from My Friends

Words and Music by John Lennon and Paul McCartney

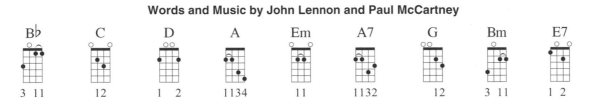

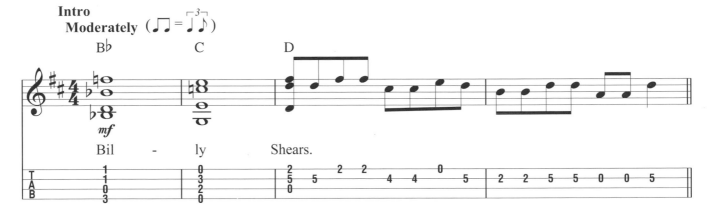

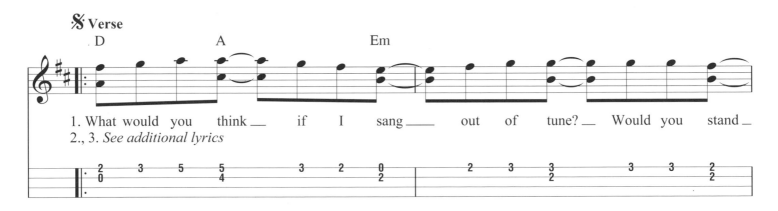

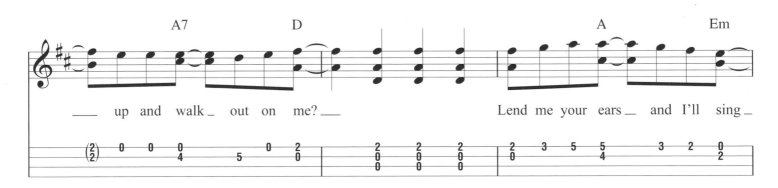

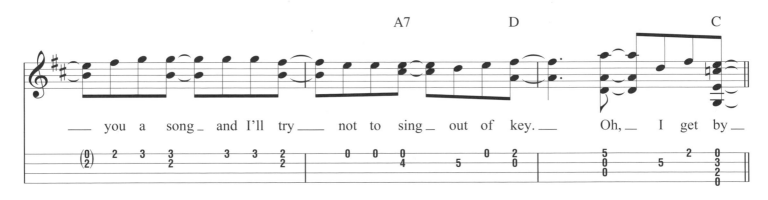

*Tremolo top note
only, throughout.

Bridge

60

Additional Lyrics

2. What do I do when my love is away?
   Does it worry you to be alone?
   How do I feel by the end of the day?
   Are you sad because you're on your own?

3. Would you believe in a love at first sight?
   Yes, I'm certain that it happens all the time.
   What do you see when you turn out the light?
   I can't tell you, but I know it's mine.

Yesterday

Words and Music by John Lennon and Paul McCartney

Intro
Moderately

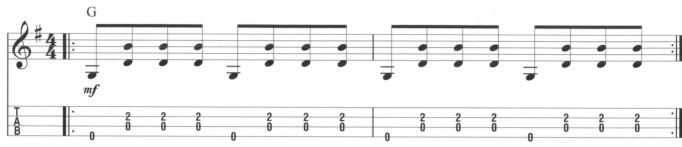

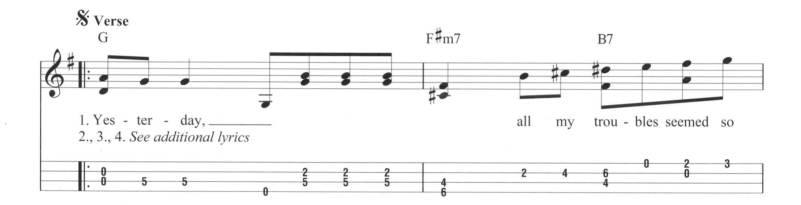

1. Yes - ter - day, _____ all my trou - bles seemed so
2., 3., 4. *See additional lyrics*

far a - way, now it looks as though they're

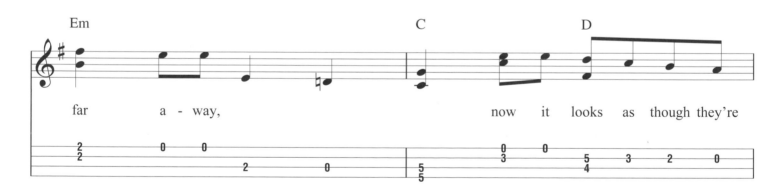

To Coda ⊕

here to stay. _ Oh, I be - lieve _ in yes - ter - day. _

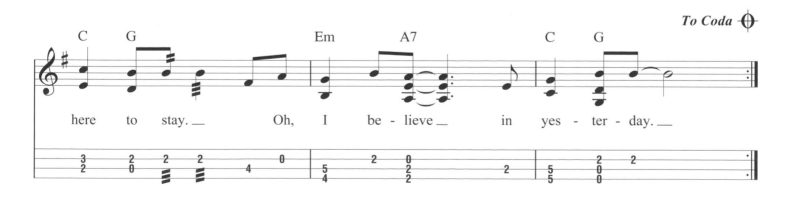

Bridge

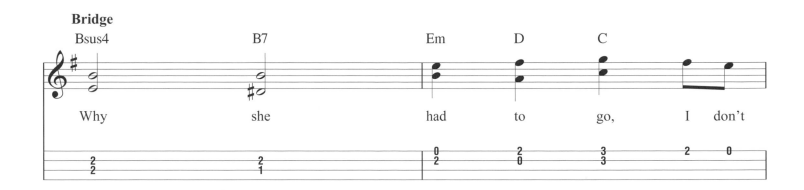

Why she had to go, I don't

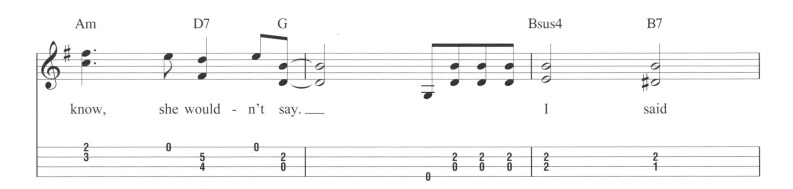

know, she would-n't say. ___ I said

1st time, D.S.
(no repeat)
2nd time, D.S. al Coda
(no repeat)

some - thing wrong, now I long for yes - ter - day. ___

Coda

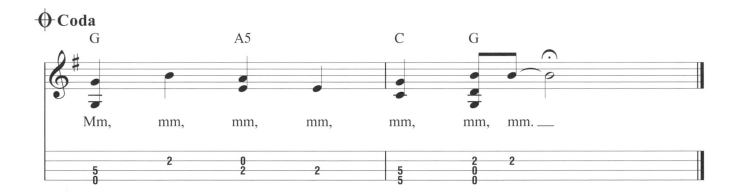

Mm, mm, mm, mm, mm, mm, mm. ___

Additional Lyrics

2. Suddenly, I'm not half the man I used to be.
   There's a shadow hanging over me.
   Oh, yesterday came suddenly.

3., 4. Yesterday, love was such an easy game to play,
   Now I need a place to hide away.
   Oh, I believe in yesterday.

MANDOLIN NOTATION LEGEND

Mandolin music can be notated three different ways: on a *musical staff*, in *tablature*, and in *rhythm slashes*.

RHYTHM SLASHES are written above the staff. Strum chords in the rhythm indicated. Use the chord diagrams found at the top of the first page of the transcription for the appropriate chord voicings.

THE MUSICAL STAFF shows pitches and rhythms and is divided by bar lines into measures. Pitches are named after the first seven letters of the alphabet.

TABLATURE graphically represents the mandolin fretboard. Each of the four horizontal lines represents each of the four courses of strings, and each number represents a fret.

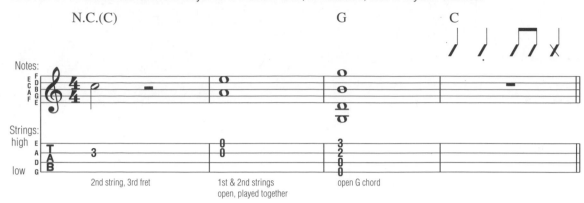

2nd string, 3rd fret | 1st & 2nd strings open, played together | open G chord

Definitions for Special Mandolin Notation

MUTED STRING(S): Lightly touch a string with the edge of your fret-hand finger while fretting a note on an adjacent string, causing the muted string to be unheard. Muting all of the strings with the fingers of the fret-hand while strumming the strings with the picking hand produces a percussive effect.

HAMMER-ON: Strike the first (lower) note with one finger, then sound the higher note (on the same string) with another finger by fretting it without picking.

PULL-OFF: Place both fingers on the notes to be sounded. Strike the first note and, without picking, pull the finger off to sound the second (lower) note.

LEGATO SLIDE: Strike the first note and then slide the same fret-hand finger up or down to the second note. The second note is not struck.

SHIFT SLIDE: Same as the legato slide except the second note is struck.

HALF-STEP BEND: Strike the note and bend up ½ step.

GRACE NOTE BEND: Strike the note and immediately bend up as indicated.

TREMOLO PICKING: The note is picked rapidly and continuously.

Additional Musical Definitions

p (piano) • Play quietly.

mp (mezzo-piano) • Play moderately quiet.

mf (mezzo-forte) • Play moderately loud.

f (forte) • Play loudly.

cont. rhy. sim. • Continue strumming in similar rhythm.

N.C. *(no chord)* • Don't strum until the next chord symbol. Chord symbols in parentheses reflect implied harmony.

D.S. al Coda • Go back to the sign (𝄋), then play until the measure marked *"To Coda"*, then skip to the section labeled *"Coda."*

D.S.S. al Coda 2 • Go back to the double sign (𝄋𝄋), then play until the measure marked *"To Coda 2"*, then skip to the section labeled *"Coda 2."*

D.S. al Fine • Go back to the sign (𝄋), then play until the label *"Fine."*

 (staccato) • Play the note or chord short.

rit.  *(ritard)* • Gradually slow down.

 *(fermata)* • Hold the note or chord for an undetermined amount of time.

• Repeat measures between signs.

1. 2. • When a repeated section has different endings, play the first ending only the first time and the second ending only the second time.

NOTE: Tablature numbers in parentheses mean:
1. The note is being sustained over a system (note in standard notation is tied), or
2. The note is sustained, but a new articulation (such as a hammer-on, pull-off or slide) begins.